The 5 Things Every Woman of-a-Certain-Age Should Have Under Her Bed

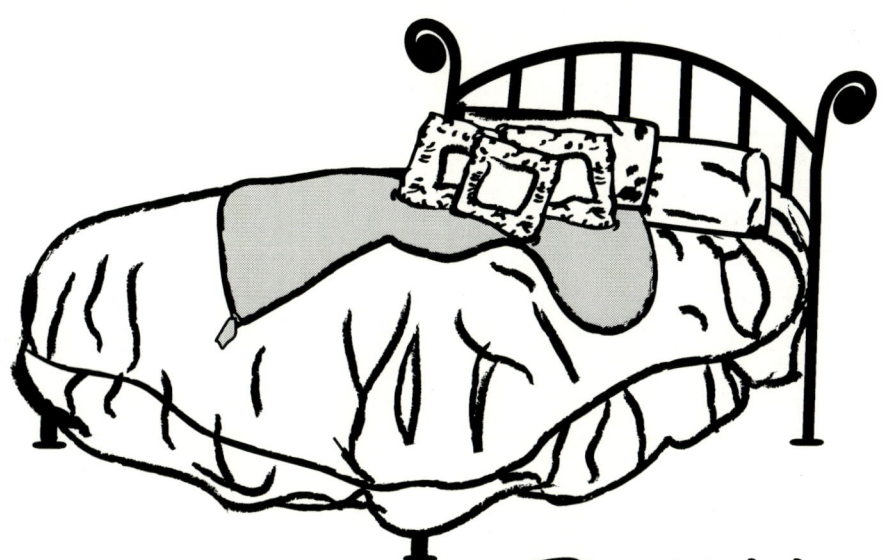

Enjoy that tingle!

Jane Thomas

Fairy Godmother
www.FairyGodmotherOnline.com

The 5 Things Every Woman-of-a-Certain-Age Should Have Under Her Bed

Copyright © 2009 by Terre Thomas
All rights reserved, including the right to reproduce in whole or in part in any form without written permission.

Restore the Tingle™ is a registered trademark of Fairy Godmother.

Illustrations and interior design by Jill Quednow
Cover design by Jennifer Closner

For speaking engagement information or for bulk discount or wholesale purchases: Call 612/825-1105 or Email: YFGodmother@aol.com

Printed in the USA.

ISBN 978-0-557-19517-6

Women Sexuality

Important note/disclaimer:
Fairy Godmother does not publish or manufacture any products recommended in this book, nor does Fairy Godmother make any warranties or guarantees about them, their use, or their effectiveness. Recommendations are solely based on the personal opinion of the author and Fairy Godmother disclaims any responsibility for any damage caused by information, or lack of information, in this book. Additionally, please forgive that partner references throughout this book are heterosexual. No excluding offense is intended to GBLT folks. I felt most comfortable writing about what I know best.

This book is in honor of all the precious moments I've had with women who went ahead and asked me the questions even though it made them blush.

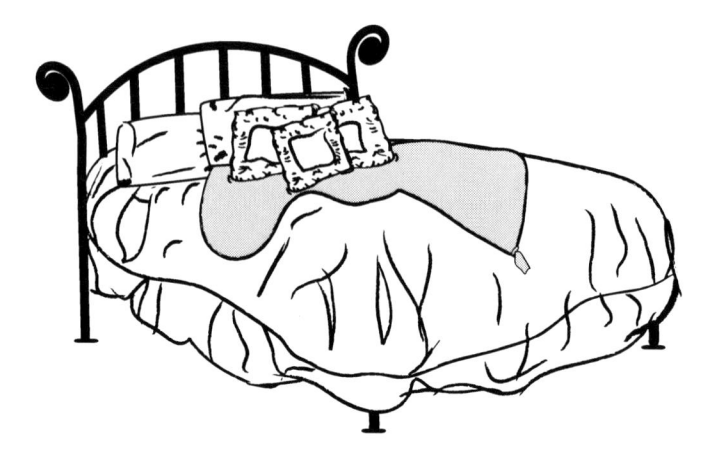

Good sex, and
more sensuous pleasure,
can fill you with energy, love,
& a terrific sense of wellbeing!

Enjoy

TABLE OF CONTENTS

PART 1: The 5 Things

The 5 Things 1
More about Each of the 5 Things 4
A Good Vibrator 11
A Good Book of Erotica 13
A Good How-To Book or DVD 25
A Good Bottle of Lubricant 31
A New Playful Erotic Accessory 35
How to Buy and Where 39

PART 2: A Bit of Fairy Godmother Wisdom

Sensuous Intelligence 45
Good Cooking & Good Sex 49
Libido Lost and Found 55
Being a Newbie 61

PART 3: Endnotes

Acknowledgements 64
About the author 65

Your tingle notes

In teaching the Restore the Tingle™ workshop, and talking with customers everyday, I've learned that for many women, learning new things about sex and sensuous pleasure can bring up a lot of old beliefs, memories, and new thoughts and ideas. So while you are reading this book, keep a pen or pencil handy and use this space to jot down notes as you go along.

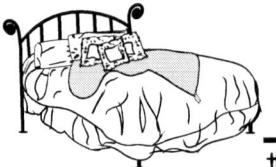

The Tingle...

...that marvelous, sexy, sensuous feeling that radiates from within.

Visit the Restore the Tingle™ department at FairyGodmotherOnline.com

Five Things?

Most women understand that for many things in life you just need the 5 basics - whether it's a good outfit, your shoe groups, your desk supplies, or your make-up... concealer, foundation/powder, blush, mascara, lipstick...and you're good to go! And at our age and with our busy lives, 5 things is about all we can remember anyway.

But when it comes to sensuous products and sex toys, not many women can tell you what the five best things are to have under your bed – and how ya gonna know? Well, I can help.

Let's face it, most people aren't fluent talking about sex and sensual pleasure. Most of us learned about sensual pleasure as teenagers and our sources were pretty shaky – television and movies, our parents maybe, and trial and error with other equally clueless teens in the backseat at the drive-in or on a couch in the basement.

With this kind of background, and the lack of everyday conversations, it's no wonder that many women don't know these 5 basics. And if you're like me, a middle-age woman of a certain age, there are probably two things that are inhibiting your sensual/sexual pleasure: your hormonally-challenged libido and a lack of knowledge about the good practical things that can help you restore your tingle.

I believe the "Tingle" is an important part of life; it's that marvelous, sexy, sensuous feeling that radiates from within. I am in the business of selling erotic accessories and books, along with a full range of other gifts for inspiration, encouragement, and fun because it all fits together – or should. I talk with women everyday who are so happy to learn that just a few good things in the sensual department can really make things better. Thanks to my years of reading, researching, and testing (often with the help of my devoted research assistant, my husband), I've figured out what the good stuff is and why and I'm delighted I can share it with you!

Your tingle notes

The clitoris, not the vagina, is the primary sensual pleasure organ for a woman.

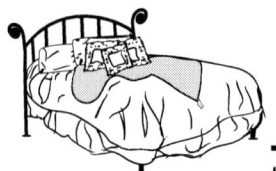

The Tingle...
...that marvelous, sexy, sensuous feeling that radiates from within.

Visit the Restore the Tingle ™ department at FairyGodmotherOnline.com

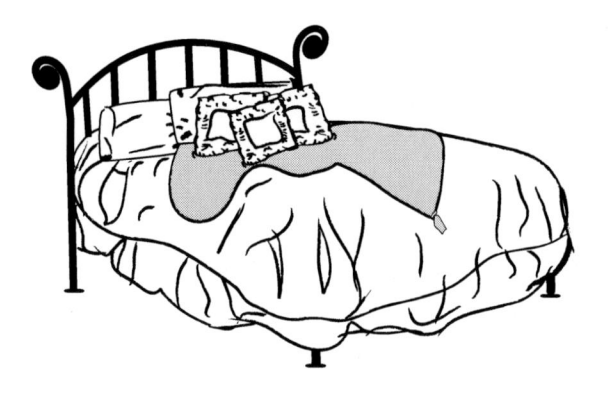

There is only one goal.

*It's not to become a wild sex kitten or cougar.
It's not to fix something that's "wrong with you".
It's not to figure out what's "normal".
It's not discovering some "Secret" that no one ever shared with you.*

The goal is simply, and sweetly, to learn, try, and do things that give you more sensuous pleasure ... more often.

So without further ado, here are the 5 things every woman-of-a-certain-age should have under her bed...

The 5 Things Every Woman of-a-Certain-Age Should Have Under Her Bed

1. A good vibrator

The clitoris is a woman's primary pleasure organ, not the vagina. With approximately 4000 lovely nerve endings densely situated in a surface area no bigger than a dime or nickel, there's nothing like the steady, consistent, intense stimulation a vibrator creates for a good orgasm. Fingers (and tongue) can find other fabulous things to do while your vibrator does its unparalleled best to create a wonderful orgasm, with or without a partner.

For more about vibrators go to page 11.

2. A good book of erotica

A good racy story can start your erotic engine and help arouse you to create a physical and emotional mood for pleasure – replacing mental chatter and other daily distractions. Since the 70's breakthrough book, *My Secret Garden; Women's Sexual Fantasies* by Nancy Friday, the genre of women's erotica has blossomed with hot, sweet, tender, funny, non-brutal erotica and there's a wealth to choose from.

For more about erotica go to page 19.

3. A good How-To Sex Information book or DVD

As I said earlier, it's safe to say that most of us got our sexual/sensual education as teenagers, and our sources were pretty shaky. Everyone has some knowledge gaps, a few questions, and probably a little anxiety about what you don't know. Fortunately, there are dozens of good books and several good DVDs out there. The trick is to find the one or two that appeal to your unique learning style, your life situation, and interests. My absolute favorite is, *I ♥ Female Orgasm* by Dorian Scott and Marshall Miller. Filling in the gaps and discovering new things can make a world of difference.

For more about how-tos go to page 25.

Visit the Restore the Tingle ™ department at FairyGodmotherOnline.com

4 A bottle of good lubricant

Even if your natural lubrication is just fine, the addition of water-based lubricant is a pleasure you don't want skip, solo or with a partner. A good lube creates a silky, slippery, friction-free sensation between body parts that want to rub together. With less estrogen, we begin to lose some muscle tone, vaginal walls begin to thin, and natural lubrication is diminished because our estrogen-dependent tissue and muscles aren't getting what they used to get; a good lubricant banishes any friction and creates a very "ahh" experience.

For more info about lubricants go to page 31.

5 A new playful erotic accessory

Trying something new can be fun and perhaps create some sensations you've never experienced. As a solo gal, it might be as simple as climbing into bed with a box of chocolates and a new book of erotica or taking a luxurious bath with a new kind of bubble bath, a water proof vibrator, and a new, really soft bath sheet (one of those big ones). For couples, it can be a feather duster, a blindfold, a deck of cards for a game of strip poker, a gift certificate for a costumed rendezvous or a scavenger hunt, or adding a vibrator or vibrating cockring to lovemaking – the possibilities are endless!

For more info on something new go to page 35.

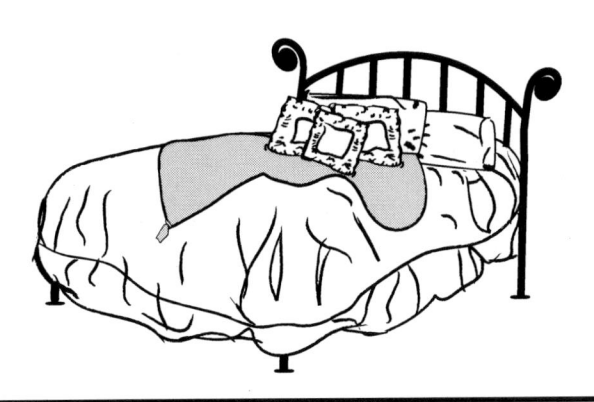

Your tingle notes

For some of us, we need to discard the notion that "good girls" shouldn't have sensual fun, which is as misguided as the argument that women shoudn't wear pants!

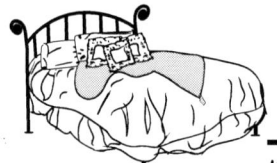

The Tingle...

...that marvelous, sexy, sensuous feeling that radiates from within.

But shouldn't this all just come to you naturally?

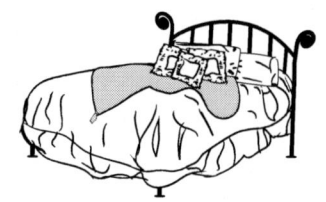

Five reasons to ignore this myth.

Experiencing more sensual pleasure is a lot like good cooking – just because you're hungry, and you need to eat, doesn't mean you naturally know how to prepare a delicious meal; and like good cooking, experiencing more sensual pleasure isn't difficult once you know the basics.

Are reading glasses unnatural? As we age, there's nothing wrong with accessories and tools that help or enhance our experiences.

Daydreams and fantasies can take you to lovely places that can fill you with creativity and well-being; there's nothing "unnatural" about that.

"Addicted" to a vibrator....well as much as you can be "addicted" to indoor plumbing, cell phones, heating and air conditioning, and other modern conveniences that create pleasure and comfort in your life.

As our hormone levels diminish and our wisdom and patience grow, we know that enjoying things, *in whatever way that works*, is important to being happy.

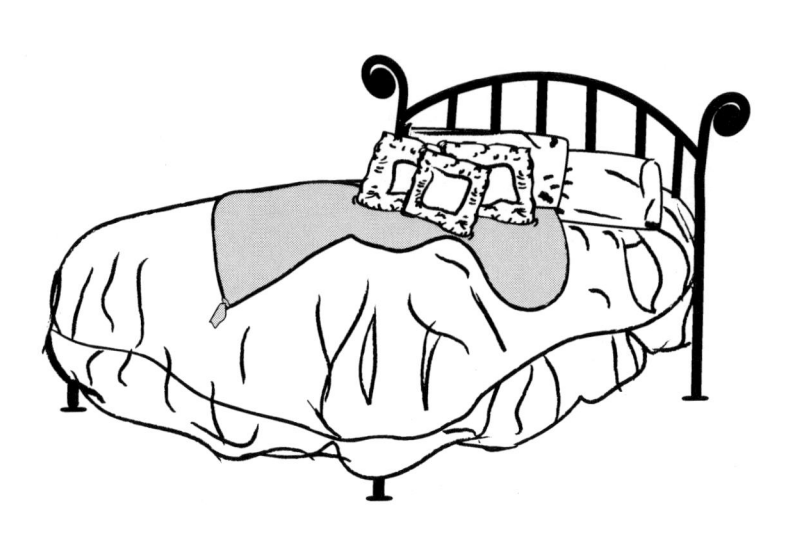

More About Each of the 5 Things...

Your tingle notes

8 out of 10 women do not have an orgasm from intercourse alone, contrary to what Hollywood depicts! The twenty percent of women who do, have nice sensitive G-Spots.

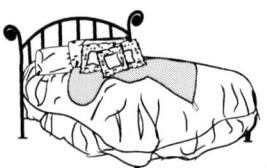

The Tingle...
...that marvelous, sexy, sensuous feeling that radiates from within.

Visit the Restore the Tingle ™ department at FairyGodmotherOnline.com

1 a good vibrator

> *"Most women absolutely require direct clitoral stimulation to achieve orgasm - and the powerful, consistent stimulation a vibrator delivers like nothing else can. The extra oomph on the clitoris that a vibrator provides is just what women need to come - whether alone or with partner."*
>
> **From Sex Toys 101, A Playfully Uninhibited Guide**
> **by Rachel Venning & Claire Cavanah**

The design and purpose of a good vibrator lets you "turn on" those 4000 clitoral pleasure nerve endings that are concentrated in such a small surface area – the size of a nickel or dime for most women. Because a man's pleasure nerve endings are spread out over a surface area vastly greater, his penis, men don't intuitively grasp (ahem) the differences in pleasure-potential between males and females with a vibrator.

Vibrators provide the kind of direct stimulation that clitoris' love and for most women, a vibrator is the sure thing - orgasm-wise; for some women it's the only way to get there! Keeping in mind that the clitoris is "command central" for pleasure, most vibrators are designed to use externally on the clit, not inside the vagina. (In my shop, the giant Hitachi Magic Wand has made many a gal's eyes go wide thinking that big thing is meant to go inside the vagina. We clear up that misconception right away.)

There are literally hundreds of choices in vibrators and lots of qualities to chose from on the market. (See page 13). But there are two important preliminary factors that you should always include in your choice: the material the vibrator is made of should be non-toxic and phthalate-free. Some softer cheaper jelly materials have a tendency to hold bacteria, even with a thorough cleaning, so check the materials. Secondly, get a vibrator that's multi-speed; our arousal cycle is multi-speed and our vibrators should be too.

Your tingle notes

Breath is an important part of having a really good orgasm. When you find yourself about to climax, don't hold your breath, instead take deep breaths and focus your attention on allowing your orgasm to spread throughout your entire body.

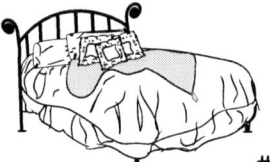

The Tingle...
...that marvelous, sexy, sensuous feeling that radiates from within.

Visit the Restore the Tingle ™ department at FairyGodmotherOnline.com

more about vibrators

There are also plenty of vibrators that are designed to put in the vagina to stimulate the G-spot and to give that nice fullness sensation. Some vibrators are dual-action, which can pleasure the clitoris, the G-spot, and the vagina simultaneously; the most famous being the Rabbit Habit with a penis-like shaft with twirling pearls that hit the G-spot while an attached little soft "rabbit" is positioned at the base of the shaft to tickle your clit. It's quite a lot of sensations going on at one time and lots of women love it.

The G-spot is a wonderfully sensitive walnut-size spot inside your vagina about two inches up along the front wall, coincidentally at the backside of those 4000 clitoral pleasure nerve endings. It's sometimes referred to as "the backdoor to heaven". When aroused, it feels a little bumpy or wrinkly and if you stroke it with a "come-hither" movement, it feels great. Many women cannot "locate" their G-spot and that's because you usually can't feel it unless you are aroused. It's the lucky 1 in 5 woman who has a super-sensitive G-spot that can have an orgasm without needing any clitoral stimulation. (Yep, 80% of us do not have intercourse-only orgasms despite what Hollywood would have us believe!)

While using a vibrator will stimulate your clitoris, it's important to understand that "getting in the tingle mood" takes more than a vibrator. You need to create a pleasure-making environment inside you head and with your body. It's time to relax, turn off the phone, light some candles, take a bubble bath, read some erotica and give yourself some undivided sensual attention.

> **Product recommendations:** Throughout this book, I do mention some of my favorite products on the market as good examples (many are classics that I hope will be around forever) but I haven't listed **all** the best ones because terrific new ones are being developed and introduced all the time! This is why the internet is so great; it's so much easier to keep information up-to-date online. So for my recommendations of the best erotic products, you can visit the Restore the Tingle department at my safe, secure, and discreet online shop, FairyGodmotherOnline.com.

5 Qualities to Consider in Choosing a Vibrator

1. **Power Source** – Plug in, rechargeable, or regular batteries, all have advantages and disadvantages. With plug-ins, you always have the reliability of a consistent power source but you are always connected to an outlet. Rechargeables are good for the environment and give you mobility to "play in the garden" wherever you'd like, unless you forget to recharge it. Most rechargeables have a back-up power source with either a cord which powers the vibrator or you can pop in regular batteries and be ready for action. Some of the higher end vibrators don't have a back-up option but will recharge within an hour. Vibrators that use regular batteries make things convenient and easy but it's a drag when the batteries run low and you didn't notice it.

2. **Ergonomics** – Consider the size, shape, weight, and ease of the controls. Vibrators come in many sizes and shapes. Most vibrators are not shaped like a penis because they are designed for external stimulation of "pleasure command-central", the clitoris. But some are specifically designed for inserting into the vagina for that nice fullness feeling and to stimulate the G-spot. The larger "massager" vibrators like the Hitachi Magic Wand and her prettier, smarter sister the Berman Center's Aphrodite are the biggest and have good motors that deliver a strong wonderful vibration but they are the size and shape of a karaoke microphone. A smaller vibrator is easier to handle but if it is too tiny it might not "feel right" in your hand. And when it comes to ease of controls, you don't want the equivalent of "programming your VCR" during an exciting moment, so if you get a vibrator with 27 programmable speeds and pulses, plan to make the time to practice and learn how to use it in rhythm with your own body.

Visit the Restore the Tingle ™ department at FairyGodmotherOnline.com

3. **Design Discretion** – Does it matter if you have a vibe that looks like a penis or do you want one that, if spotted by your kids or your mother, will not be easily identified as a sex toy? Or do you just want a pretty one? The Hitachi, Aphrodite, and Acuvibe vibrators are also well-known as great shoulder and neck massagers, so that's kind of a good multi-purpose disguise. Some look like beauty appliances and some are like little pieces of art.

4. **Power of the Vibrator** – If it's your first "real" vibrator, you need to consider how sensitive your clitoris is and think about the amount of manual stimulation that you need to reach orgasm. If you aren't sure, or haven't had a strong orgasm before, choose a vibrator with a stronger vibration because you can always "mute" a vibe through clothing, blanket/sheet, or towel but you can't do much with a vibrator that's too weak. In my experience, it's the less expensive vibrators under $50 that don't have a "strong enough" vibration, although some, like the one-speed Berman Center's Athena, have a strong vibe, but they are usually noisier and less smooth running. The motor on vibrators differ with sound and smoothness (oscillation) while running. I really believe it's true that the more you spend on a vibrator, the better the quality.

5. **Cost** – A well-made, multi-speed vibrator will cost $50-$100+. It really is a "you get what you pay for" product because higher quality materials, mechanical design and function, and a good motor will simply cost you more. The more you spend, the more features and the higher the quality of the vibrator. Because I test all the vibrators for Fairy Godmother, I love many of them but I believe the Fun Factory *Layaspot* vibrator is the currently the best value vibrator under $100 on the market. Buying a cheap vibrator is like buying cheap electronics. I also want to encourage you to buy from reputable businesses that are committed to providing information and products with integrity, not just the lowest price.

Your tingle notes

How to say it? Clitoris: KLIT-uh-rus or kli-TORE-us. It's a lot like tom-A-toe or tom-ah-toe; both work.

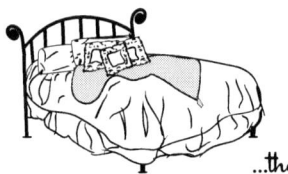

The Tingle...

...that marvelous, sexy, sensuous feeling that radiates from within.

Replacing your honey... I don't think so!

One concern I hear about vibrators is, "How can I make sure my man doesn't feel like he's being replaced by a machine?"

For starters, we know that no piece of plastic or silicon with a motor can deliver a deep warm kiss or lightly brush or nibble a nipple or the inside of your thigh. A vibrator cannot whisper your name, grab you passionately by the kitchen sink, or hold you tenderly under the covers. So, you have to address the concern with sweet talk, information, and maybe a present!

Here's some talking points that may be helpful:

- *Honey, I was reading this fun little book about sex written by a fairy godmother and she says that every woman ought to try a vibrator with her husband/boyfriend/partner when they are having sex because...*

- *...apparently you and I both have about 4000 pleasure nerve endings "down there" but your 4000 are spread out all over your penis and my 4000 are concentrated in the area no bigger than a nickel or dime – my clitoris – so a vibrator works on me in a way that you just couldn't imagine....*

- *The fairy godmother also said that there's a thing called a vibrating cockring that will give you a taste of vibrating pleasure AND because it lines up, when you are wearing it during intercourse, with my clitoris, it's a pleasure for me too.*

- *Now, let me tell you, I know that no little vibrator could ever replace how much I love being kissed, touched, and _____ (fill in the blank yourself) by you, but I think adding a vibrator to our love life might be really fun.*

Your tingle notes

Self-pleasure, we like to call it "roaming in the garden", is good for your long-term health because it keeps the juices flowing and the muscles working. It's good excercise.

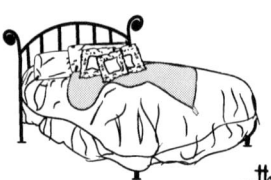

The Tingle...

...that marvelous, sexy, sensuous feeling that radiates from within.

Visit the Restore the Tingle ™ department at FairyGodmotherOnline.com

2 a good book of erotica

Good erotica depends on the story's ability to arouse at the right pace. A good erotic story needs to be like any good story, crafted with good characters, an imaginative plot, an interesting setting, and especially descriptive language. With good erotica, the descriptive language has to both be explicitly descriptive enough guiding the reader to their own arousing images in the mind and libido. Good erotica must also have a length and pace that stimulates a reader's natural arc of arousal.

Speaking of arousal, many women-of-a-certain-age find with diminishing hormonal levels that desire and arousal often require a jump start and erotica is a great one. A good erotic story can get your tingle going much like the aroma of delicious food, when you walk into the kitchen, can trigger your appetite even when you didn't "think" you were hungry. So if you find that you want or need to treat yourself to some sensual pleasure but you aren't quite "in the mood", try scheduling a date with a good book of erotica to reawaken your dozing tingle. Erotica can also be a powerful type of foreplay, helping your body and spirit get in the mood before a romantic encounter with your lover – and maybe contribute a couple ideas for new things to try.

Most books of women's erotica are collections of stories by a variety of authors with different themes and styles. If you haven't read much erotica or discovered what's exciting to you, the best place to start is *My Secret Garden; Women's Sexual Fantasies* by Nancy Friday. *My Secret Garden* is not a collection of fiction erotica but rather a collection of over two hundred real women's fantasies. The scope of fantasies in *My Secret Garden* is so great that it would hard not to find the kind of stories that you find arousing. The only downside to *My Secret Garden* (and sequel *Forbidden Flowers*) is some of the fantasies are only 2-3 paragraphs long and that's not long enough for arousal-friendly pacing (and be advised that a handful of fantasies include abduction, rape, or sex with animals...but not many). Fortunately, most women's erotica is written without including brutality or violence and it's tailored to a woman's sensual sensibilities.

Your tingle notes

"Masturbation" is such a boring, multi-syllabic word for such a nice activity. Here are some more fun phrases for it: *roaming in the garden, jilling off, menage á moi, polishing the pearl, and paddling the pink canoe.*

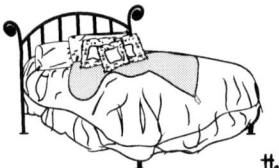

The Tingle...

...that marvelous, sexy, sensuous feeling that radiates from within.

Visit the Restore the Tingle ™ department at FairyGodmotherOnline.com

more about erotica

Once you have a sense of the kinds of stories you like, look for collections that have many of those types of stories. Realize, also, that something you and your body find arousing in a story or fantasy doesn't mean you would actually want to do it – any more than enjoying a good murder mystery or scary movie means you'd like to murder someone.

You can't always guess which story, or kind of story, will excite and arouse you, and because most collections cover a wide range, some you'll like, some not. The key is to find enough that do.

When you are reading through an erotica collection, mark the stories that make you tingle, and the next time skip the ones that don't work. Not every collection will do it for you but you'll find certain themes that you like and discover certain erotica editors whose tastes and quality standards work for you.

Our best selling favorite is *Five Minute Erotica; 35 Passionate Tales of Sex and Seduction* edited by Carol Queen. There's a great range of types of stories in it, no brutality, and because they are shorter, they are great for read-alouds with a partner. Editors Alison Tyler and Tristan Taormino all have quite a few good collections and Cleis Press (CleisPress.com) offers the widest selection of good quality erotica on the market. Unfortunately, good audio books of erotica are few and far between. Hopefully that place in the market will blossom more in the future.

> **Product recommendations**: Throughout this book, I do mention some of my favorite products and resources on the market as good examples (many are classics that I hope will be around forever) but I haven't listed **all** the best ones because terrific new ones are being introduced all the time! This is why the internet is so great; it's so much easier to keep information up-to-date online. So for my recommendations of the best erotica, you can visit the Restore the Tingle department at my safe, secure, and discreet online shop, FairyGodmotherOnline.com.

Your tingle notes

The average amount of stimulation time "from start to orgasm" for women is twenty minutes; the average for a man is two to five minutes. Explains a lot, right?

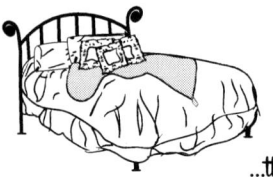

The Tingle...

...that marvelous, sexy, sensuous feeling that radiates from within.

Visit the Restore the Tingle ™ department at FairyGodmotherOnline.com

a note about erotic movies

As for erotic movies, they are not really made for a female audience and that's because experts say that women are more "romantically aroused" and men are more "visually aroused", this explains why men don't seem to mind the missing plot or the mediocre "acting" and production quality. It also explains why many women find that the tingle just doesn't get tingling while watching one. But give us a steamy "romantic" scene in a movie and that tingle perks right up. So, my best advice for a movie turn-on is to find a mainstream movie that makes you hot. If you can't think of a favorite, I recommend an internet search of "SEXIEST MOVIE SCENES" and there are links to dozens of sites that recommend the best of sexy, romantic scenes and movies.

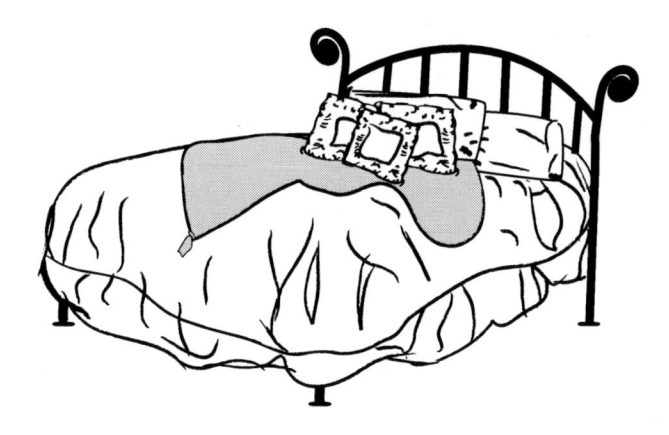

Your tingle notes

Why didn't formal sex education ever include mention of the clitoris or orgasms? Hmmmm?

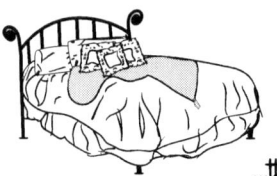

The Tingle...
...that marvelous, sexy, sensuous feeling that radiates from within.

Visit the Restore the Tingle ™ department at FairyGodmotherOnline.com

3. a good how-to book or dvd

Most of us got our formal sex education (if we got any at all) from school presentations that were clinical and were essentially an anatomy lesson with a heavy dose of instilling the fear of unplanned pregnancy. I've yet to meet a woman whose sex ed class even mentioned an orgasm or the clitoris.

Informally, it wasn't much better. As I mentioned earlier, most of our informal sex and sensual education came from television and movies that erroneously depict women experiencing fabulous orgasms through intercourse alone (which, in reality, happens for about one in five women). And then of course, we relied on our goofy teenage friends and sweethearts for the trial and error "hands-on" training, usually in the backseat of a car. Many of us have spent years letting our "inner teenager" run our sex lives.

Consequently, we all have gaps in our knowledge with sex and sensual basics. How could we not!

Fortunately, we now have the time, maturity, and interest in finding new and better ways to enjoy our bodies. And we have much better resources to fill in the gaps with accurate, appropriate, and up-to-date information.

Because sex education, aka "sex talk" has a tendency to overwhelm anyone, whether you are twelve years old, twenty-five, or fifty-five, I believe the best sex books are the ones that are written with information in small kiss-size bits (like this book) and don't read like a medical text book or PhD thesis.

And there are now books that are written with more specific audiences and topics in mind. There are books for single women, for couples keeping their sex life alive while raising kids, for people with chronic illness or disability who want a good sex life, for women who've experienced sexual trauma, lesbian and gay sex books, sex books for women over sixty and lots more.

Your tingle notes

Name some masterful sensual/sexual qualities or skills you possess. Are you a terrific kisser? Do you do something with your fingernails that drives your lover wild? Are you great with shared or solo fantasy? With your sultry voice, can you seduce with a few well chosen words by phone?

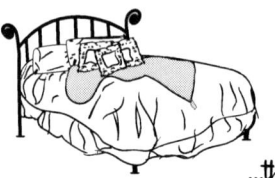

The Tingle...

...that marvelous, sexy, sensuous feeling that radiates from within.

Visit the Restore the Tingle ™ department at FairyGodmotherOnline.com

more about how-to books & dvd

There are also specific topic books about sex toys, vibrators, anal sex, oral sex, how to talk dirty in different languages, erotic massage, tantric sex, and a host of books on different positions.

If your learning style is better with DVDs, there are a few good sex info DVDs but the production quality in this industry is not great. It's less like the Discovery channel and more like good community cable production. So keep that in mind if watching-to-learn is your preference.

The Sinclair Institute's *The Better Sex Series: Sexplorations* and *The Couples Guide to Great Sex Over 40* are two of the best, combining information, couples actually talking about sex in a way you can learn from and imitate, and then the couples get naked and demonstrate more positions and activities than you could ever imagine. Men, who are more visually aroused, like the demonstration part and women, who are more romantically aroused, like the couples-talking part; good bits for both of you! With a bottle of wine, it's the makings for a good date that could benefit you both for a long time.

Product recommendations: Throughout this book, I do mention some of my favorite products on the market as good examples (many are classics that I hope will be around forever) but I haven't listed **all** the best ones because terrific new ones are being developed and introduced all the time! This is why the internet is so great; it's so much easier to keep information up-to-date online. So for my recommendations of the best erotic products and books, you can visit the Restore the Tingle department at my safe, secure, and discreet online shop, FairyGodmotherOnline.com

Fairy Godmother's top recommendations

I ♥ Female Orgasm!
by Dorian Solot and Marshall Miller
I honestly believe this is the best sex book ever written. It's informative, funny, interesting; it's presented like one of those women's magazine that's filled with interesting, *useful* information that you can put to use immediately. I wish everyone on the planet, women and men, would read this book.

Sex Toys 101; A Playfully Uninhibited Guide
by Rachel Venning & Claire Cavanah
Loaded with wonderful, useful information by weaving funny stories, sex facts that you know you "ought" to know, and endless possibilities and suggestions for using sex toys in your life. A great way to learn lots more about sex and sex toys and to perhaps prompt a discussion with your partner about trying something new: "Look at this! Can you believe it! Think you'd ever want to try it?"

Better Than I Ever Expected; Straight Talk about Sex After 60
by Joan Price
Sexuality advocate Joan Price knows that many women over sixty are having the best sex of their lives. By sharing personal stories of her own and those of the sexually seasoned women, she gets personal and stays positive, offering ways to overcome physical challenges, bump up the excitement, and unlock joyful sensuality with a partner, or on your own, during the golden years.

Sexy Mamas; Keeping Your Sex Life Alive While Raising Kids
by Cathy Winks & Anne Semans
Mothers know that sexuality doesn't disappear when kids arrive; it get buried under laundry, fixing dinner, carpool schedules, and conflicting demands. Sexy Mamas offers great practical advice and strategies to reclaim it, like how to "have it all- sex, sanity, and sleep"!

Visit the Restore the Tingle ™ department at FairyGodmotherOnline.com

for the best How-To's

The Ultimate Guide to Sex and Disability: For All of Us Who Live with Disabilities, Chronic Pain, and Illness
by Miriam Kaufman, M.D., Cory Silverberg, and Fran Odette
For everyone, men and women of all ages and sexual identities, this book covers the span of disabilities with the overall message: there is no "right way" to have sex. Individuals can affirm what 'sex' is for them and give themselves permission to consider anything as a sexual experience.

Better Sex Series: Sexplorations DVD
From The Sinclair Institute
The *Better Sex Sexplorations* DVD provides great basic sex information, show couples talking about sex (not an easy thing for many couples), and then the couples get naked and demonstrate it all. This DVD caters to men's arousal through the "visual" (the nude couples demonstrating) and women's arousal through the "romantic and conversational" (dressed couples having great, candid conversations). The topics and positions are wide-ranging and it's guarenteed to fill in some of the missing pieces and information gaps for anyone!

Sexplorations: Couples Guide to Great Sex Over 40 DVD
From The Sinclair Institute
The *Couples Guide to Great Sex Over 40* also provides great basic sex information, show couples talking about sex (more mature couples dressed and talking about it all), and then the couples (with real-life middle-age bodies) get naked and demonstrate it all. My husband and I appreciated the non-model bodies and the great examples of conversations between couples about many things we hadn't been very comfortable talking about. The best message in the DVD is "yes, everything does slow down when you hit middle-age but there can be a lot more pleasure in the slowing down".

Your tingle notes

As women begin to have diminishing hormone levels with estrogen, progesterone and testosterone during peri-menopause, it affects vaginal elasticity and lubrication, pelvic muscle strength, and sexual desire (libido).

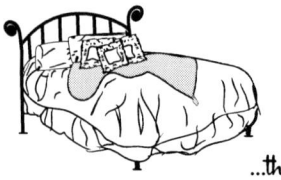

The Tingle...

...that marvelous, sexy, sensuous feeling that radiates from within.

Visit the Restore the Tingle ™ department at FairyGodmotherOnline.com

4 a bottle of good lubricant

Water-based sexual lubricant should win an Oscar for best-supporting role in sex! It'll never be the star of the show but good lube can make a performance simply great.

As we get older, our estrogen levels drop and our vaginal walls begin to thin and natural lubrication decreases. For some women, it makes intercourse painful and a good sexual lubricant may be a good simple solution to the common problem*.

Even if you have no problem with natural lubrication, a good lubricant ensures that two surfaces rubbing against each other will glide, not create friction. So whether it's your partner's parts, your solo fingers, or your favorite sex toy, use lubricant to heighten your pleasure to an "ahhh" level when contact happens.

Lubricants come in the water-based and silicone-based variety. Water-based, glycerin-free** lubricant is the best all around choice because it is compatible with the vagina, anus, condoms, and sex toys made of silicone and it's easy to clean-up.

Most water-based lubricants become tacky after a while when the water is absorbed into your skin but you can make them slippery again by spraying with a mister. Or you can use the Fairy Godmother favorite, Liquid Silk, which stays slippery far longer than any others because it has a drop of silicone and best of all, instead of becoming tacky when it dries up, it absorbs beautifully into your skin. It's a little more expensive than many lubricants but it is totally worth it. Liquid Silk does contain propylene glycol, so if you have sensitive skin, use an all-natural lubricant and just remember the mister trick when it gets tacky. Also, a small drop of lube inside the tip of a condom, before it's put on, helps create a better sensation for him…but just a drop because too much lubricant could cause condom slippage.

Your tingle notes

Diminishing estrogen impacts the bladder, urethra, and vagina. Vaginal tissure lining can go from a thickness of forty layers to four during peri-menopause.

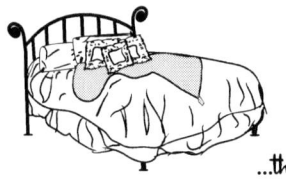

The Tingle...

...that marvelous, sexy, sensuous feeling that radiates from within.

more about sexual lubricants

Silicone-based lubricant is best for anal sex. It's thicker and longer lasting than water-based lube but it does not absorb into the skin, so it doesn't clean up with soap and water and therefore it's not good in the vagina. Silicone-based lube is not compatible with sex toys made of silicone because the toy will degrade with contact with the lubricant.

But for anal penetration, whether it's for his pleasurable prostate stimulation or your pleasure, silicone lube's great texture and long lasting staying power provide great needed lubrication because the anus does not naturally produce any lubrication. Through natural elimination, silicone lubricant will clean out of the anus just fine.

Many lubricant lines sell one-time packets and small travel-size bottles, so try a couple different types to see which lubricant you'd like to be the best supporting character in your next passionate act.

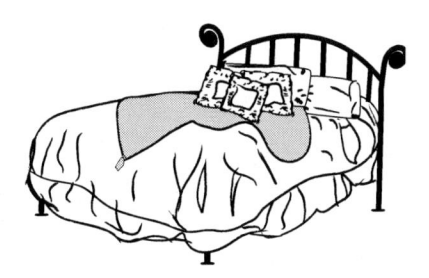

*Diminishing estrogen levels create vaginal dryness for many of us and if a sexual lubricant isn't enough, talk with your healthcare provider about other treatment options like the Estring, an estradiol vaginal ring, other bio-identical hormone replacement therapies, and alternative treatments.

**Lubricants with glycerin, which is sugar, can encourage vaginal yeast infections. Flavored lubricants also usually contain sugar, so if you are susceptible to yeast infections, check the ingredients listed on the packaging.

Your tingle notes

Masturbation, or as we prefer to call it, *roaming in the garden*, is a great way to build your sexual confidence and it will create better orgasms for you, either alone or when you are with a partner.

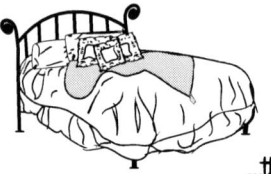

The Tingle...

...that marvelous, sexy, sensuous feeling that radiates from within.

Visit the Restore the Tingle ™ department at FairyGodmotherOnline.com

5 — *a new playful erotic accessory*

Solo Fun

Why should that tingly radiance and lovely sense of well-being only be a partner-dependent experience? Solo sensual pleasure puts a twinkle in your eyes and a sparkle in your energy level. And regular orgasms keep the juices flowing and keep all your equipment in working order. Staying sensually fit is an important part of staying physically fit.

Adding something new to your sensual menu is like discovering a new favorite treat to eat; cream cheese-stuffed French toast with praline sauce at Famous Dave's BBQ is my latest. So try a new book of erotica that has a theme you like, or get a waterproof vibrator and take a candle lit bath, rent a sexy movie and splurge on chocolate or champagne, or both!

The simple act of exploring to find something new affirms that you are a sensuous being who stays in touch with the pleasure of her body. Remember, the only goal is to have more sensual pleasure...more often.

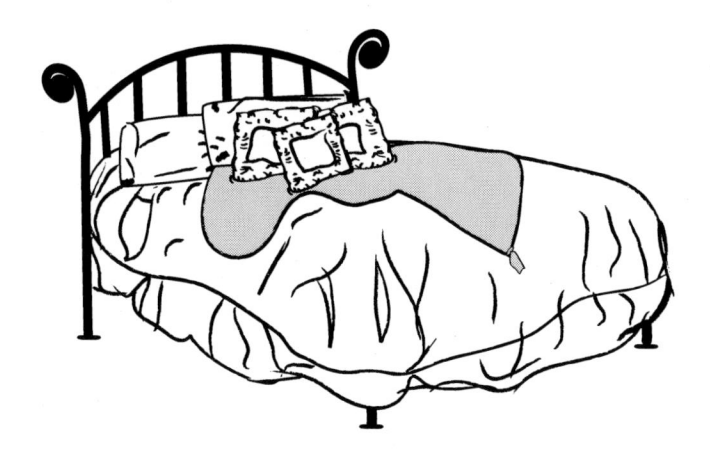

Your tingle notes

If you've been with one partner for years, you've probably had sex hundreds, or even thousands, of times... how could it not become somewhat "routine", like brushing your teeth. Trying something new doesn't mean you haven't been satisfied, it just means that you want to try a new flavor of toothpaste.

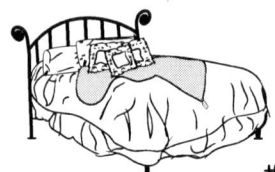

The Tingle...

...that marvelous, sexy, sensuous feeling that radiates from within.

Visit the Restore the Tingle ™ department at FairyGodmotherOnline.com

more playful erotic accessories

Partner Fun

In my Restore the Tingle™ workshops, I almost always get the question, "How am I going to get my husband to try something new?" My response is a good wifely one: In plenty of areas of your couple-life you often "make" him do things that are good for him, or both of you, right? Less ice cream, more frozen yogurt, less red meat, more chicken or fish, less TV, more exercise. So why not "more sex but with some new kinds of fun, honey"? I have yet to hear any man complain about more sex, even if he has to try something new to experience it.

Never tried erotic massage? Get an erotic massage DVD and a good bottle of massage oil. Try out any of the delicious recipes from *Intercourses; An Aphrodisiac Cookbook* by Martha Hopkins & Randall Lockridge and serve dinner in a negligee. Or get one of the many fun sex coupon books, split it in half and alternate gift giving and receiving from week to week.

Trying something new doesn't necessarily mean you haven't been satisfied, it's more like you've decided to be a better "cook" in the bedroom. (See Good Cooking & Good Sex on page 49) So shake it up, mix it up, add something new to your repertoire – the Tingle awaits you!

Product recommendations: Throughout this book, I do mention some of my favorite products on the market as good examples (many are classics that I hope will be around forever) but I haven't listed **all** the best ones because terrific new ones are being developed and introduced all the time! This is why the internet is so great; it's so much easier to keep information up-to-date online. So for my recommendations of the best erotic products, you can visit the Restore the Tingle department at my safe, secure, and discreet online shop, FairyGodmotherOnline.com

Your tingle notes

In a study about vibrator use among women, as reported in the Journal of Sexual Medicine, researchers at Indiana University's Center for Sexual Health Promotion surveyed 2,056 women found that more than half of the women (52.5 percent) had used a vibrator, with nearly one in four having done so in the past month and that vibrator use was positively related to several aspects of sexual function (desire, arousal, lubrication, orgasm, pain and overall function) with recent vibrator users scoring themselves higher on most sexual function domains, suggesting more positive sexual function.

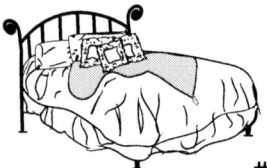

The Tingle...

...that marvelous, sexy, sensuous feeling that radiates from within.

how to buy and where

Like technology, the erotic accessories market for women is growing like mad and making its way into the mainstream. As the market grows, it makes the products more accessible, makes the manufacturers create better quality products, and with the internet, allows us to be better consumers because we can do research on the products, and learn what some of them are for! (I'll never forget my first "buying trip" to a trade show in Las Vegas, wandering the aisles as a distinctly Midwestern middle-age mom/lady, trying to figure out exactly what-the-heck some of those things were supposed to do.)

It's true that there are still some of the old school sleazier elements present in the industry, and probably always will be. Some of the materials and ingredients are bad for you, some of the products are cheaply and poorly made, and some of the vendors may not be scrupulous about your privacy if you buy online, so it's important to be a savvy consumer while having fun finding the right fun products.

Here's what I suggest:

*Do your research to determine what you want to buy, or at least narrow down the type of product you're interested in and the most important characteristics you'd like.

*Go online and search "product review of _____". There are quite a few sites with people who've shared their opinions and experiences. A set of reviews of some vibrating panties once saved me from throwing away $100.

*Ask someone whose judgment you trust for recommendations and advice. "Barb, do you know anything about picking out a good vibrator?"

Your tingle notes

In a study about vibrator use, as reported in the Journal of Sexual Medicine, researchers at Indiana University's Center for Sexual Health Promotion surveyed 2,056 women and 1047 and found that a couple's vibrator use during sex play is common, with about 45 percent of men and 53 percent of women, ages 18 to 60, reporting such.

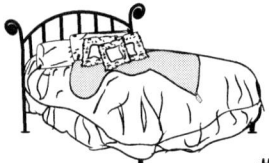

The Tingle...

...that marvelous, sexy, sensuous feeling that radiates from within.

Visit the Restore the Tingle ™ department at FairyGodmotherOnline.com

where to buy

Once you have a pretty good idea of what you want, here are some options of where to buy:

*A reputable online store (like FairyGodmotherOnline.com). A great place to find a trustworthy women-friendly online shop is to check the resource lists in most of the How-To books I've recommended. If you shop Amazon.com, be sure to click on the actual vendor who will fulfill your order and then decide if you want to order from them.

*A sex toy store. Some cities have women-friendly stores and the best way to find them, again, is look in the resources section of the How-To books or use the internet. Many of the major cities, San Francisco, Berkely, Madison, Ontario, Chicago, Minneapolis and many college towns have sex toy shops that are welcoming, well lit, and have well-trained staff to answer questions. If you do go to a traditional sex toy store and you have a good idea of what you are looking for, you probably will find a selection of products that will include better quality products to choose from. You can think of it as a raunchy date or a "field trip" to a foreign place.

*Sex toy parties. These parties are fun because you get to interact, ask questions, and touch and turn on the products. The downside is that you may not want to host or attend a party in order to buy what you'd like.

*Mainstream stores. Target and some of the national chain drugstores are expanding into this market. The selection is still pretty limited, and products are often in the same aisle as tampons, hairspray, or deodorant, so you really need to know what you are looking for because the stock boy sure won't be able to answer any questions.

Just remember you're simply trying new things to enhance your sensual pleasure and there's lots to choose from. So, relax, give it a try and have fun.

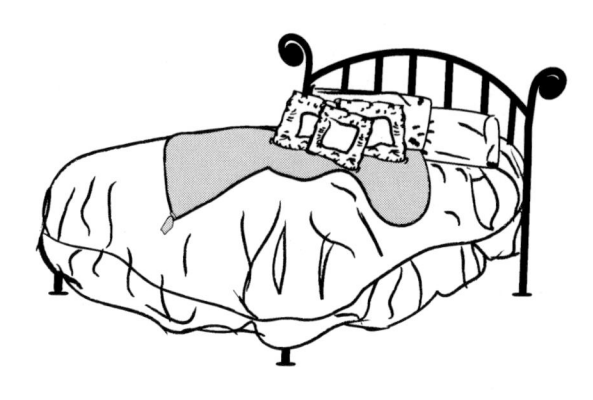

A bit of Fairy Godmother Wisdom

Your tingle notes

Flashback exercise: Think back to a time in your past when you know you were wildly attractive. What were you wearing; what were you doing; where were you? Try to physically recapture the memory with your body.

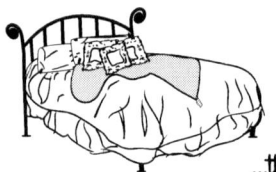

The Tingle...

...that marvelous, sexy, sensuous feeling that radiates from within.

Sensual Intelligence

I appreciate the concept of "Multiple Intelligences" which creates a framework that acknowledges giftedness in areas besides pure logical intellect. Conceived by Howard Gardner, there are seven types of intelligences: visual, verbal, logical, bodily, musical, interpersonal, and intrapersonal. I believe that an eighth one should be added to the list, "sensual intelligence".

Some people are just more sensually gifted; and like the other intelligences, they were probably born with it. They have no doubt been in touch with their sensual side since they were young. Maybe the numbers are higher than I think (because in our culture most people are shy about explicitly revealing how sensual they are) but in my fairy godmother capacity, women share a lot with me and my staff and there are some women who clearly just have an easy and natural perspective about their bodies and their own pleasure.

But just like those who have a great intellect or extraordinary artistic talent, it is not as common as our Sex In The City younger sisters, and most advertisers, would have us believe. It's just that so many "public people" and experts seem to be so crazy about it – with the suggestion that if you're not, something is wrong with you.

Does this mean that those of us who haven't luxuriated in sleeping naked since we were girls should settle for a life of lackluster physical pleasure? Heck no. No more than we should toss our books and journals, paintbrushes, guitars and pianos, or yoga mats and running shoes because we're not rock stars, professional athletes, or Pulitzer winners.

One of the beauties of being human is our capacity to learn things and stretch into new facets of ourselves. I often liken learning to enhance sensual pleasure to learning to be a good cook. Just because you're hungry doesn't mean that you naturally know how to prepare a delicious meal, but with good recipes, ingredients, and time in the "kitchen", you can be. (See Good Cooking & Good Sex on page 49)

Your tingle notes

It's easy to notice the lovely, sexy, enviable qualities in others, right? Take a moment right now, step outside yourself and name three sexy qualities you possess. Your sparkling eyes, beautiful fingers, a cute butt in jeans. Come on, you can come up with three!

1. _____
   _____

2. _____
   _____

3. _____
   _____

The Tingle...
...that marvelous, sexy, sensuous feeling that radiates from within.

Visit the Restore the Tingle ™ department at FairyGodmotherOnline.com

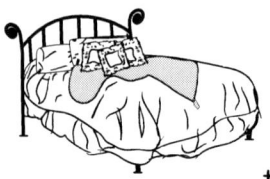

Sensual Intelligence

Those of us who are not naturally "sensual genii" can to do a couple of things to become more skilled at sensual pleasure:

1. Recognize that those who are fluently sensual/sexual are the ones who are most visible and pubic about it and we can ignore the implication that there is something inadequate about us just because we are not as naturally gifted as they are.

2. Commit to learning more about what pleases you sensually and sexually. Sensual/sexual pleasure skills are something most of us didn't get much training in, but that doesn't mean you can't learn more, and try more, starting now!

3. Realize that it takes a time commitment to raise your sensual IQ, just like learning any new thing. As we get older, there aren't a lot of new things that have to learn. As women-of-a-certain-age, we have mastered a lot of things and being a "newbie" can be an unfamiliar and uncomfortable experience but you just have to get over it. The key is to study, learn, and practice, practice, practice.

4. Use external resources. Vibrators, erotica, and lubricants can greatly enhance sensual pleasure; and helping find the right ones for you is the reason I've written this book. Think of a good vibrator like a good pair of reading glasses – it helps with focus!

5. Ask questions and talk about it with your lover and with your friends. If you need some help getting started, take this book in hand and use it as a conversation starter - "Look at this fun book I just picked up! Have you ever played with a vibrator? Do you have a favorite book of erotica?" Have you ever used a feather duster as a sex toy?"

Make it fun, make it funny, and it's okay if you blush. There's nothing to lose except your limitations and there's nothing to gain but more pleasure!

Your tingle notes

Joke: A woman is in a bar with girlfriends and she spots an incredibly handsome man and she can't help but stare at him. After a few moments, the man walks over to her and whispers to her, "I will do anything, absolutely anything for you, no matter how kinky, for $20 if... you can describe it in just three words. With her heart pounding, the woman thinks for a moment, then slowly pulls a $20 from her purse, gazes deeply into the man's eyes and says...

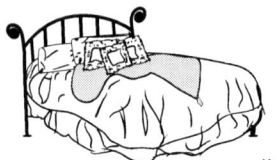

"Clean...My...House"

The Tingle...

...that marvelous, sexy, sensuous feeling that radiates from within.

Visit the Restore the Tingle ™ department at FairyGodmotherOnline.com

Good Cooking & Good Sex

A few years ago I came up with a darn good metaphor for good sex, or more accurately, learning how to get better at sex. It's cooking!

Every day in my shop, and especially during our Restore the Tingle™ workshops, I tell women that learning to enhance sexual pleasure has the same elements of learning to be a good cook. Think about the similarities.

First, with sex, there's this widely held notion that because you have innate desire, you automatically, or "naturally" know how to do it well. But just because you're hungry doesn't mean you know how to make a delicious omelet.

As a beginner in cooking, one needs **basic information** - knowledge of how to work the stove, which things need to be kept cold/hot, and basics like "why pre-heat the oven" and why cooking something over a maximum flame doesn't necessarily make it cook faster or taste better. (Are you seeing some good sex equivalents here?)

With sex, for most of us, that basic information didn't come from a patient grandma or mom in the kitchen. No, most of us got a bit of training from orgasm-free sex-ed at school, parents, or church or in the backseat of a car at the drive-in. And then we rounded it off with TV and the movies and we know how realistic and accurate that can be! In fact, my "favorite" TV/movie sex myth is that all women have orgasms during vaginal intercourse (with no other stimulation) when, in fact, only one in five women do! Yep, 80% of us have orgasms only with clitoral stimulation…but every beauty on screen has been feeding us (and all the men) the baloney that we should naturally be having orgasms by intercourse alone. Aargh!

Sexually, a lot of the basic information is the same as it was 10, 20, 30, 40-some years ago but everyone has some missing gaps, and there are a lot of really great new things that have appeared in the world of erotic enhancements (like great water-based, glycerin-free lubricant) that are worth learning about and the safer sex stuff is critically important for all you gals who have re-entered the dating world.

Your tingle notes

How do you like to be told you're attractive?

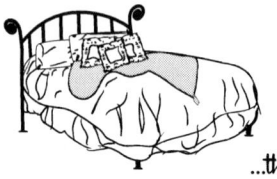

The Tingle...
...that marvelous, sexy, sensuous feeling that radiates from within.

Visit the Restore the Tingle ™ department at FairyGodmotherOnline.com

Good Cooking & Good Sex

Describing what you like

There are some wonderful, informative, tasteful audios and DVDs that can teach everyone a valuable new thing or two. (The Sinclair Institute's *The Couples Guide to Great Sex Over 40* DVD is excellent.)

Next, is the **vocabulary,** the right words, to describe the processes and equipment: boil, sauté, sift, whip, fry, froth. (I guess many of these could be sex words too.) With sex, when we are learning about the basics, we have the medical and slang terms, but regardless of word choice, most of us rarely have a good situation in which to practice actually saying them aloud, or heaven forbid, asking questions about them.

"I think I prefer my eggs over easy, not scrambled. I want to try both to see which I like best," is much easier than, "I think I prefer my nipples to be sucked, not bitten and I think I want to try both right now."

My favorite passage in Carol Queen's *Five-Minute Erotica's* short story, Captain, May I? by Elise Matthesen, is when the woman say to her lover, "How can I talk about sex to you when I can't talk about it in the privacy of my own head?" Her resourceful lover then produces a vocabulary-building list of "ways to please your lover" for them to read aloud.

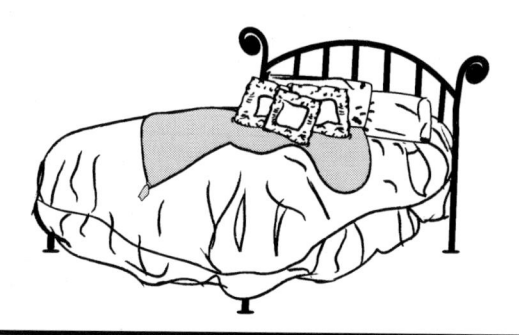

Your tingle notes

it is rare that two people's sexual appetites are going to be in perfect synch, so put a little more energy into finding out the colliding sweet moments of opportunity and desire.

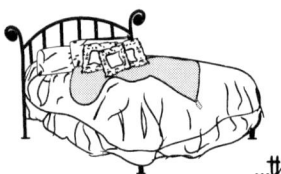

The Tingle...
...that marvelous, sexy, sensuous feeling that radiates from within.

Visit the Restore the Tingle ™ department at FairyGodmotherOnline.com

Good Cooking & Good Sex

Then there are the **recipes**. Even if you aren't a cookbook reader, you can be a decent cook if someone shows you how to prepare a lovely meal.

With sex, some of us have been fortunate to have "stumbled" across someone who taught us some recipes for pleasure that went beyond our backseat or television/movie sexual education. And some of us are more sensually-gifted, and through self-exploration, learned the personal secrets to more pleasure, but lots of us didn't. Fortunately, instructions, the recipes for physical delight are available, just like cookbooks, through erotica and how-to books, like *Sex Toys 101*, *The Ultimate Guide to Sex and Disability*, *The Good Vibrations Guide to Sex* or my personal favorite, *I♥ Female Orgasm!*.

Lastly, all good mature cooks know that having a kitchen stocked with high-quality **ingredients, equipment and tools** is important to culinary pleasure and success. And under the bed is no different than in the fridge or cupboard. Think good olive oil and good lubricant. Think Kitchenaid mixer and a good powerful vibrator. I also think reading glasses are another great metaphor for the enhancing power of a vibrator, as we need a little boost to help with the "fine print" of our bodies' responsiveness.

While it has been amusing, and hopefully illustrative, the most powerful point of the "Good Cooking – Good Sex" metaphor is that to be good at either.... to have pleasurable results.... you need to devote time and attention to it. You have to **practice, practice, practice** in order to master the skills that will lead you to an experience so succulent it melts in your mouth.

Your tingle notes

Distraction, fatigue, and preoccupation are culprits that'll rob you of pleasure. Be a super heroine and banish them with loving attention, rest, and a commitment to focus on your pleasure.

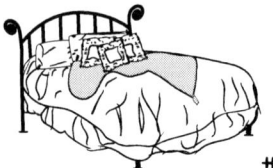

The Tingle...

...that marvelous, sexy, sensuous feeling that radiates from within.

Visit the Restore the Tingle ™ department at FairyGodmotherOnline.com

Libido Lost & Found

Libido n. (lĭ bĕ'dō) *1. the psychic and emotional energy associated with instinctual biological drives 2. a. a sexual desire b. manifestation of sexual desire.*
The Free Dictionary

As we mature into this "certain age", it's a time in life that brings more freedom – freedom from birth control (or at least the end is in sight), more free time because kids don't require as much of your energy and attention (hopefully), more money to spend on ourselves, and thankfully, more patience and maturity about what's important and what's not.

It's a developmental stage that gracefully asserts, "Oh yeah, I'm going to make the time for *me* now, finally!" and more sensual pleasure and good sex are at the top of the list (or in the top 5).

For some, great sensual pleasure has been only an occasional friend over the years – an experience that usually took a backseat to carpool responsibilities, a briefcase of work brought home, laundry, yard work, school science projects, and on and on and on.

For others, it's never had a chance to blossom in the first place...for whatever reason.

But now with the time, the space, the resources, the wisdom, and the desire to claim (or reclaim) your libido, your hormones come along and let the air out of your tires....right when you're ready to take off down the road to pleasure. Damn!

Can the changes in three chemicals in our body, estrogen, progesterone, and testosterone, really spoil it? Sure, they've got your libido trapped in the "Lost and Found" closet! And to get it back, you're going to need a strategy.

Your tingle notes

Testosterone is the hormone of desire for women. There's only a small amount in our system compared to men but when it decreases, so does our libido.

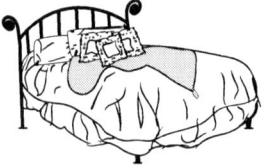

The Tingle...

...that marvelous, sexy, sensuous feeling that radiates from within.

Visit the Restore the Tingle ™ department at FairyGodmotherOnline.com

Libido Lost & Found

Each and every woman has both a unique history and a unique chemistry at this stage of life and everyone's path to pleasure is equally unique but I believe there are three components that make up the solution for every woman.

1. A commitment to figuring it out.
As caretakers and nurturers we, ironically, don't always do a good job taking good care of ourselves – no surprise there. But for this issue, no one else has a better view of what's off-kilter and what will work for you *than you*; not your health care provider, not your sister or mom, not your best friend. They can help with insight and knowledge but you must devote real time and attention to identifying and learning about what's going on with your body and your sexual desire and explore the options to make it right.

2. Finding and choosing the best hormonal support for you.
There are lots of options to choose from: bio-identical hormone replacement therapy, synthetic hormones, "natural" herbal treatments and remedies, lifestyle and nutritional changes, and more. The choices are vast and the relief is worth it. It's also important to be open and flexible about changing and adding new solutions as you go through different phases of hormonal changes.

3. Using your head and other resources for a jumpstart.
For many women, once aroused, the road to pleasure is just fine but the "desire" to get started is what's lagging – that's testosterone not doing its job (yes, we women have and need it too). Fortunately the brain can step in and take over. My best advice is – pour yourself a glass of wine and tell your body a good story, through erotica or a sexy movie; it will do wonders to physically jumpstart your tingle engine. Arousal has physical, chemical and mental components and you need to intentionally fire up all three to make the magic happen.

Your tingle notes

As men age, they too experience diminished sexual "oomph". At age 20, it takes a man 5 seconds to get an erection, at age 50 it takes an average of 30 seconds, at age 70, it takes 6 minutes.

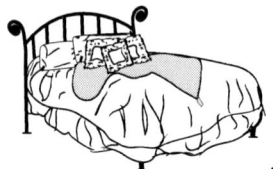

The Tingle...

...that marvelous, sexy, sensuous feeling that radiates from within.

Visit the Restore the Tingle ™ department at FairyGodmotherOnline.com

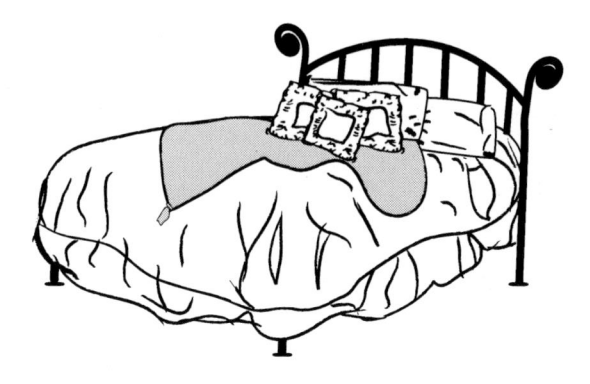

The libido isn't just influenced by hormones, it is powered by psychic and emotional energy and while we can't control the drops and fluctuations in our hormone levels, we can gather and focus our psychic and emotional energy and embrace the freedom and pleasure of this "certain age".

Your tingle notes

This week, dress to accentuate your unique loveliness.

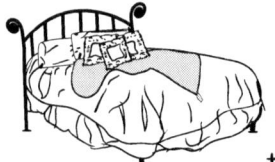

The Tingle...

...that marvelous, sexy, sensuous feeling that radiates from within.

Visit the Restore the Tingle ™ department at FairyGodmotherOnline.com

Being a Newbie

How do you learn new things?

My youngest daughter recently got her driver's license and I was reminded of how overwhelming it can be to process something new - physically, visually, spatially, and logically - simultaneously! At our age there aren't many things we haven't mastered (except maybe the new technology stuff) and therefore being a "newbie" at something can be anything from unfamiliar to distinctly uncomfortable. So, when was the last time you had to learn a new thing?

Whether it's using a vibrator for the first time, or talking about sex in a new way with your partner, or trying a little costume role playing, it's important to remind yourself that being new at something is just that – being new at it. With patience, a sense of humor, and practice, practice, practice you'll get better and you'll move to proficiency, on your way to mastery.

When I first started selling vibrators in my shop in Minneapolis, I had a woman come in who had purchased one a few weeks earlier, and she confided to me that she felt kind of clumsy and awkward with her new vibrator. I asked her to think back on when she got her first cell phone and had to learn to use it. "It took practice, right? And you got better with it, didn't you?"

Most people don't like to feel silly or incompetent and some dislike it so much that they'd rather abandon trying and learning something new than feel anything but less than masterful. But trying new things is the hallmark of a woman who has the courage and moxie to add good new things to her life when the time is right.

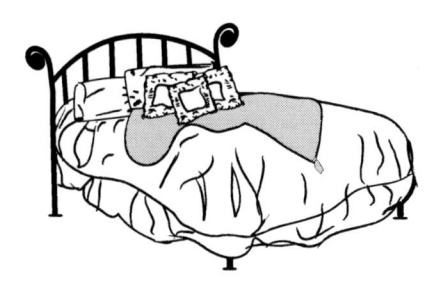

Remember, there is only one goal.

It's not to become a wild sex kitten or cougar.
It's not to fix something that's "wrong with you".
It's not to figure out what's "normal".
It's not discovering some "Secret" that no one ever shared with you.

The goal is simply, and sweetly, to learn, try, and do things that give you **more** sensuous pleasure ... **more** often.

I hope you've enjoyed this book! I always love to see who helped the author make it happen, so here are my heartfelt thank you's:

Thank you Jill Quednow, my Fairy Godmother/Restore the Tingle partner-in-crime, for your hard work, talent, enthusiasm, commitment, and faith, especially the faith, in what we do - in our ballgowns!

Thank you Bill Radosevich, my husband and devoted Tingle "research assistant", for your unflagging support for all my endeavors, your money, and for always "seeing" and loving me.

𝒯erre 𝒯homas is a self-proclaimed fairy godmother who believes the purpose of life is to make the world a better place...and have fun while you do it. For her, she's been doing both as owner of FairyGodmotherOnline.com and Fairy Godmother, a gift shop in Minneapolis that specializes in books and gifts for inspiration, encouragement and fun. Part of the fun part is the Restore the Tingle™ department which features women's erotica and erotic accessories (sex toys). The Restore the Tingle™ department and Restore the Tingle™ workshops that she teaches inspired her to write this book. She wears a ballgown to work everyday.

Terre also has fun with her husband, grown children, grandchildren, and friends in Minneapolis. She also loves to sneak away to Isla Mujeres in Mexico as much as she can.